T0390023

Silver**Tip**

Valleys and Gorges

by Ashley Kuehl

Consultant: Jordan Stoleru,
Science Educator

BEARPORT
PUBLISHING

Minneapolis, Minnesota

Credits

Cover and title page, © [Hans Henning Wenk]/Getty Images; 3, © Ruslan Suseynov/Shutterstock; 5, © Calvin Chan/Shutterstock; 6–7, © Marco Zeppetella/Alamy Stock Photo; 8, © Tim Roberts Photography/Shutterstock; 9, © kavram/Shutterstock; 11, © Fogey/Shutterstock; 13, © Simon Dannhauer/Shutterstock; 14–15, © pichetw/Shutterstock; 17, © vwalakte/iStock; 19, © Jordan Michael Anderson/Shutterstock; 21, © Regine Poirier/Shutterstock; 23, © Yakov Oskanov/Shutterstock; 24–25, © weltreisendertj/Shutterstock; 27, © MARK GARLICK/SCIENCE PHOTO LIBRARY/Getty Images; 28, © Christos Georghiou/Shutterstock.

Bearport Publishing Company Product Development Team

President: Jen Jenson; Director of Product Development: Spencer Brinker; Managing Editor: Allison Juda; Associate Editor: Naomi Reich; Associate Editor: Tiana Tran; Art Director: Colin O'Dea; Designer: Kim Jones; Designer: Kayla Eggert; Product Development Assistant: Owen Hamlin

Statement on Usage of Generative Artificial Intelligence

Bearport Publishing remains committed to publishing high-quality nonfiction books. Therefore, we restrict the use of generative AI to ensure accuracy of all text and visual components pertaining to a book's subject. See BearportPublishing.com for details.

Library of Congress Cataloging-in-Publication Data

Names: Kuehl, Ashley, 1977– author.
Title: Valleys and gorges / By Ashley Kuehl.
Description: Minneapolis, Minnesota : Bearport Publishing Company, [2025] | Series: Earth science-landforms: need to know | Includes bibliographical references and index.
Identifiers: LCCN 2024007954 (print) | LCCN 2024007955 (ebook) | ISBN 9798892320542 (library binding) | ISBN 9798892325288 (paperback) | ISBN 9798892321877 (ebook)
Subjects: LCSH: Valleys–Juvenile literature. | Gorges–Juvenile literature.
Classification: LCC GB561 .K84 2025 (print) | LCC GB561 (ebook) | DDC 551.44/2–dc23/eng/20240222
LC record available at https://lccn.loc.gov/2024007954
LC ebook record available at https://lccn.loc.gov/2024007955

For more information, write to Bearport Publishing, 5357 Penn Avenue South, Minneapolis, MN 55419.

Contents

A Tiger Leaps

The rushing Jinsha River flows between tall mountains. Legends say a tiger once jumped across this river. It leapt over the water at the bottom of the gorge to escape a hunter. This story gives the narrow, deep cut its name. It is known as Tiger Leaping Gorge.

Tiger Leaping Gorge is about a million years old. Humans may have been living in the area as far back as 15,000 years ago. Some left behind ancient drawings and tools in caves near the river.

Tiger Leaping Gorge can be found in the Yunnan province of China.

Valley or Gorge?

There are a few different kinds of valleys. But any long, narrow strip of land that sits lower than the land on both sides of it is called a valley.

These **landforms** can be shaped like a V or a U. Some valleys fall between hills or mountains. Others cut through plains.

The Great Rift Valley is about 4,000 miles (6,400 km) long. Though it's broken into parts, this is the world's longest valley. It starts in the Middle East and stretches down the eastern side of Africa.

Gorges are types of valleys. What sets these valleys apart? All gorges cut between hills or mountains. They are V-shaped and have steep, rocky sides. There is always a river flowing along the bottom of a gorge.

A canyon is another kind of valley. It also has steep, rocky sides and a river running through it. However, this landform is wider than a gorge.

Washing Away Rock

Many valleys are formed by rivers. A river's flowing water breaks off bits of rock or dirt in its path. This is called **weathering**.

The water carries away those pieces in a process called **erosion**. Eventually, so much rock and dirt wash away that it leaves behind a valley.

As winter changes to spring, mountain snow melts. This can add lots of water to a river all at once, causing floods. Flooding can make erosion happen faster.

Ice can change the shape and size of valleys. Giant sheets of ice known as glaciers slowly move across land. As they go, glaciers rub against the ground below them. If a glacier flows through a valley, it smooths out the land. The valley becomes U-shaped.

Water can get into cracks in a gorge's rocky walls. The water **expands** if it freezes. This can break apart the rock. Erosion washes these bits of rock away. The gorge becomes wider.

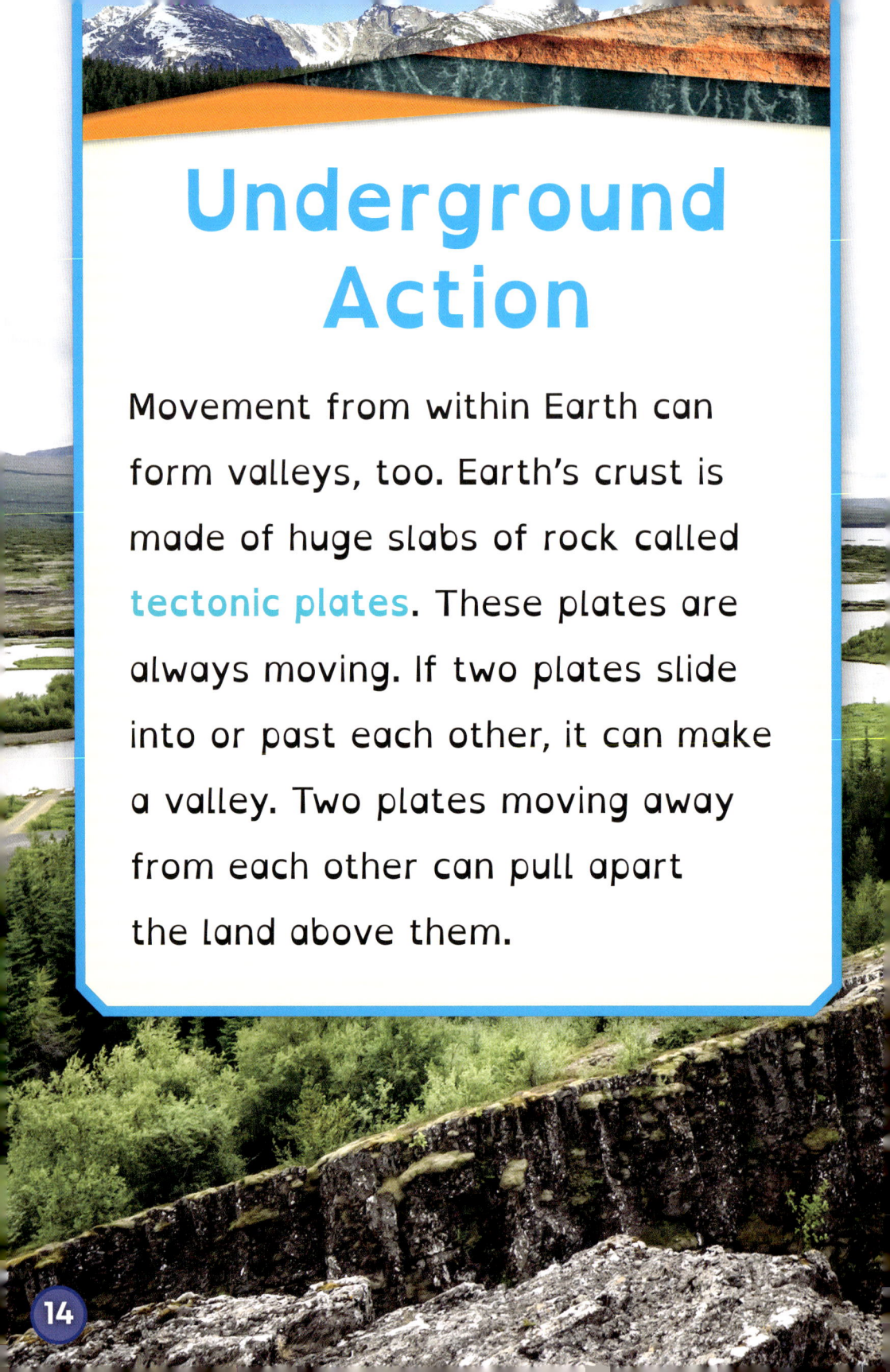

Underground Action

Movement from within Earth can form valleys, too. Earth's crust is made of huge slabs of rock called **tectonic plates**. These plates are always moving. If two plates slide into or past each other, it can make a valley. Two plates moving away from each other can pull apart the land above them.

Valleys made when plates pull apart are called rift valleys. They can form on land as well as along the ocean floor. The Mid-Atlantic Ridge has rift valleys that are 9 miles (15 km) wide along the ocean floor!

Hard Rock and Soft Rock

Valleys are always changing. Water and ice can keep breaking off bits of rock. So can wind. This makes valleys grow. Valleys with faster or bigger rivers grow more quickly.

The type of rock in a valley can also affect how it changes. Softer rock washes away more easily.

Sandstone is a soft rock. The weathering and erosion of this rock can make very narrow and deep valleys. They often have smooth sides. These are called slot canyons.

Wind can carve irregular shapes into slot canyons.

Water Storage and Electricity

Some people have found ways to use these natural wonders. People build **dams** to stop river water from flowing through the landforms. The valley becomes a **reservoir**. It holds the water. Then, people can use the water for drinking or farming when they need it.

Flaming Gorge Reservoir in Green River, Wyoming, holds water thanks to a dam. People drink the water. They also swim, boat, and fish in the reservoir.

Flaming Gorge Reservoir

Controlling the water moving through a gorge can also help make electricity from flowing water. Holding lots of water in a dam builds pressure. When the water is let out, it flows quickly. The movement spins a turbine, which runs a generator. This makes electricity.

Hydropower is a clean source of energy. It does not let out pollution. But blocking waterways can cause other problems. It may harm animals living in the area. People often have to move, too.

Ancient Layers of Rock

Scientists learn a lot about history by studying valleys. Rocks often build up in layers over thousands or millions of years. The different layers can tell us about what was happening at the time they formed. Looking in a valley can show many layers at once.

Olduvai Gorge shows layers of rock that are 2.1 million years old! Fossils from some of the earliest humans have been found at the gorge. They have helped us learn how humans changed over time.

Olduvai Gorge

23

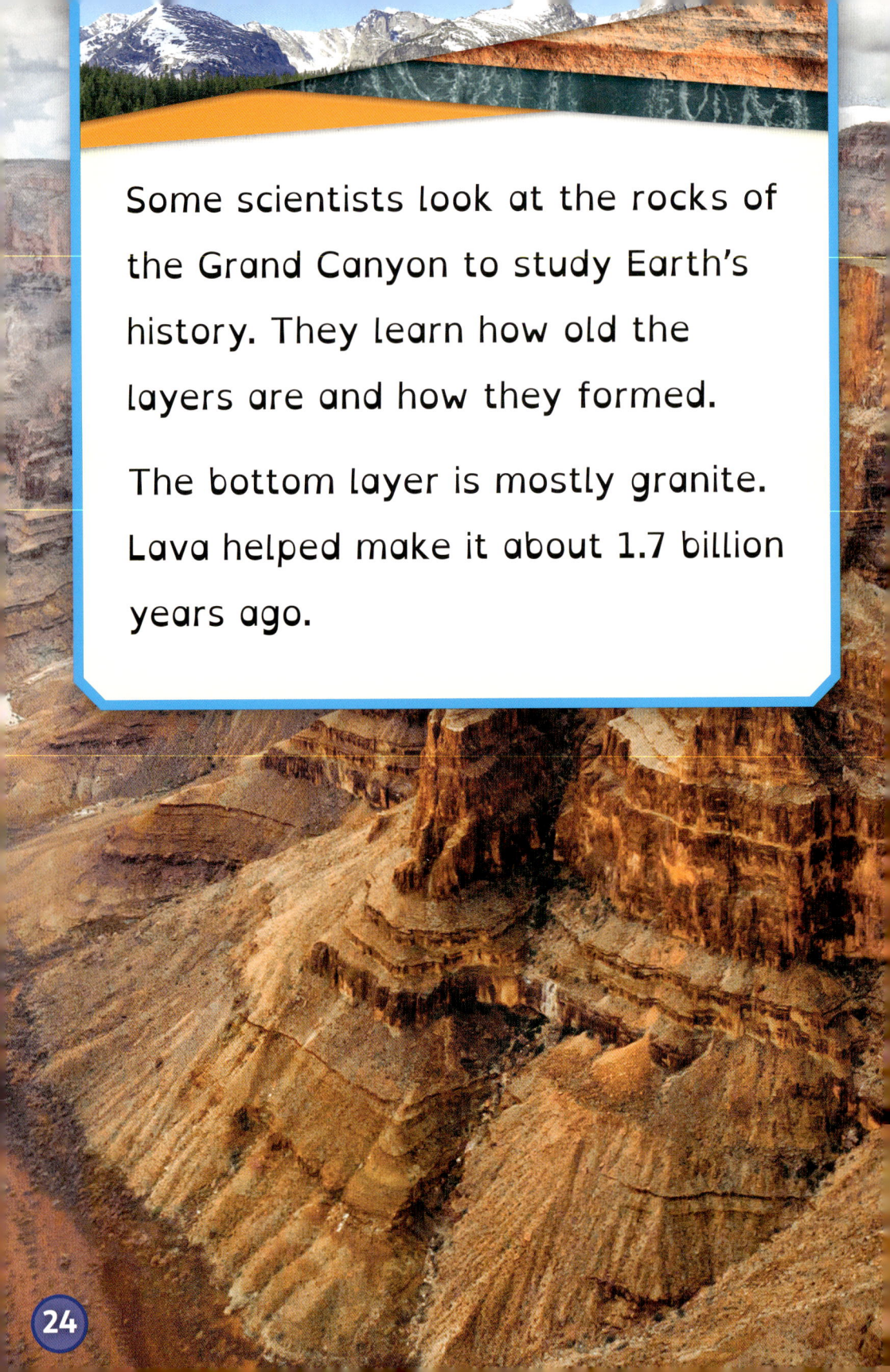

Some scientists look at the rocks of the Grand Canyon to study Earth's history. They learn how old the layers are and how they formed.

The bottom layer is mostly granite. Lava helped make it about 1.7 billion years ago.

The layers at the top of the Grand Canyon are the newest. But even these rocks are old. Scientists believe they formed more than 300 million years ago.

Learning from Landforms

Valleys can even teach us about the history of other planets. Mars has the biggest canyon in our solar system. It is about 6 miles (10 km) deep. This gives scientists a peek into the Red Planet's past. We can learn a lot by looking into valleys on Earth and beyond.

The deepest valley on Mars is called Valles Marineris. It is about 2,500 miles (4,000 km) long. Scientists guess movement of the planet's tectonic plates probably formed the canyon. Water may have helped.

Valles Marineris on Mars

Rivers Shape Valleys

Rivers can carve valleys into flat land.

A river flows across land. The water breaks off and washes away some of the dirt and rock underneath it.

If the river keeps flowing in the same area, it carves away more dirt and rock. A valley begins to form.

As time passes, a river valley can become even deeper. If it is carved out with V-shaped sides, it can become a gorge.

★ SilverTips for REVIEW

Review what you've learned. Use the text to help you.

Define key terms

canyon   gorge

dam   weathering

erosion

Check for understanding

What are the key features of a valley. Describe what makes a valley a gorge or canyon.

What forces can form a valley?

How do people use valleys?

Think deeper

In what ways do valleys affect your life? How about the lives of other people?

★ SilverTips on TEST-TAKING

- **Make a study plan.** Ask your teacher what the test is going to cover. Then, set aside time to study a little bit every day.

- **Read all the questions carefully.** Be sure you know what is being asked.

- **Skip any questions** you don't know how to answer right away. Mark them and come back later if you have time.

Glossary

dams strong walls built across rivers or streams to hold back water

erosion the carrying away of rock and soil by natural forces, such as water and wind

expands takes up more space

generator a machine that creates electricity

landforms natural features on Earth's surface

pollution harmful materials that make air, water, or land dirty

pressure the force made by pushing on something

reservoir a human-made lake created to store fresh water

tectonic plates huge pieces of rock that make up the outer crust of some planets

turbine a machine with paddles that is powered by moving water

weathering the breaking apart or wearing away of rock and soil by natural forces, such as water and wind

Read More

Emminizer, Theresa. *Water and Rock: How the Grand Canyon Formed (Earth's History through Rocks).* New York: PowerKids Press, 2020.

Leaf, Christina. *Grand Canyon National Park (U.S. National Parks).* Minneapolis: Bellwether Media, 2023.

Mihaly, Christy. *Energy from Water (Energy for the Future).* Lake Elmo, MN: Focus Readers, 2022.

Learn More Online

1. Go to **www.factsurfer.com** or scan the QR code below.

2. Enter "**Valleys and Gorges**" into the search box.

3. Click on the cover of this book to see a list of websites.

Index

About the Author

Ashley Kuehl is an editor and writer specializing in nonfiction for young people. She lives in Minneapolis, MN.